LENNY THE LION

WRITTEN BY JOHN STORMS
ILLUSTRATED BY ROBERT STORMS

HEIAN

© 1994 Text by John Storms
Illustrations by Robert Storms

ISBN: 0-89346-799-5

Heian International
1815 W. 205th St. Ste.# 301
Torrance, CA 90501

First printing 1994

94 95 96 97 98 10 9 8 7 6 5 4 3 2 1

Printed in Hong Kong

 Hi! My name is Lenny, and I'm a lion.

Like most lions, I live in Africa. There you can find mountains, jungles, and broad grasslands called savannas. Lions like to live in the savannas where there are thorny bushes and clumps of acacia trees. These make great hiding places and perfect spots for taking a nap.

Do you know any of the nicknames for lions?

Sometimes I'm called "Lord of the Jungle." But that's pretty silly because I don't even live in the jungle!

I'm also called "King of the Beasts." That's funny too. After all, I don't live in a castle, and I sure don't wear a crown on my head! Gosh, you can't be a king without a crown!

2

My friends call me "Racer." That's my favorite nickname, because I love to run races with my friends. Do you like to race too?

There's only one friend that I've never been able to beat. His name is Charley, and he's a cheetah. Charley is not even half my size, but is he ever fast!

I'm a lot bigger and stronger than Charley. Why, I'm almost nine feet long from the tip of my nose to the end of my tail, and I weigh more than five hundred pounds.

I can run faster than 35 miles per hour-- that's pretty fast, don't you think?

But Charley runs over 50 miles per hour! Can you believe it? No one can run faster than Charley.

Charley may be fast, but I'm better looking than he is. After all, I have a long, beautiful mane. Charley doesn't even have a mane, only spots. Do you know what a mane is? It's the circle of long hair that grows around my head and neck. Doesn't it look great? Only male lions have manes-- females never do.

Not only is my mane beautiful, it also protects me. Whenever I play with my friend Olivia the ostrich, she pecks me right on top of my head. If I didn't have my long, thick mane to protect me, I sure would have a headache!

My mane is just perfect...except for one thing. Everything gets stuck in it! Sometimes my mane is so full of grass, sticks and leaves that I look like a walking haystack! Then all the other animals laugh at me--especially Louie the laughing hyena. It's **SO** embarrassing! It makes me wish I could just disappear......

Hey! Where am I? Have I disappeared? Not really! All I did was crouch down in the tall grass and stay very still. My tawny coat is the same color as the pale yellow grass of the savanna, and when I lie down, you just can't see me.

But lions always know how to spot other lions in the grass. All we do is look for black dots! The tips of our tails are black and so are the backs of our ears. This is a **BIG** secret that I'm sharing with you, so please don't tell anyone else! Otherwise, we wouldn't be able to hide from anybody anymore.

YAWN!!! After all this talking, I'm getting sleepy. I'll bet that I take more naps than you do. I usually sleep more than 20 hours every day! Do you think that's a long nap? I don't. Sometimes I stretch out in the shade of a tree. Sometimes I curl up in the tall grass, next to a waterhole.

Other times, I pretend I'm a monkey. I climb up a low tree where I fall asleep on a big, wide branch.

That's really comfortable...except for the times when I roll over and ....
WHOOSH..BAM!!!
I fall right out of the tree!

13

Uh oh...now I've done it! I woke up my whole family! A lion family is called a "pride." Members of a pride live in the same territory, but we don't spend all of our time together. Our territory can be over 100 square miles in size, so we don't always see one another every day.

How do you suppose we talk to each other when we're miles apart? We don't use a telephone. We don't use a radio. We just **ROAR!!!!!** My roar can be heard over five miles away! Shhh...I think I hear my friend Lynette calling me to dinner. Our favorite food is meat. Lynette and the other female lions do almost all of the hunting.

What do I do? Well, I spend most of my time guarding our territory. That makes me so hungry that sometimes I think that I could eat a whole herd of elephants! Well...on second thought, maybe not!

Uh oh! There goes my buddy Leroy to dinner.
I'd better hurry--he eats everything!

I just had a great idea! Would you like to come visit me in Africa? I'd be glad to teach you how to roar...imagine how surprised your mom and dad would be! Pack your bags and come on over--we'll have a roaring good time out on the savanna!